SCRIPTURAL NOVENA
TO SAINT JOSEPH

The Holy Family

Scriptural Novena to Saint Joseph

Most Rev. Arthur J. Serratelli
S.T.D., S.S.L., D.D.

CATHOLIC BOOK PUBLISHING CORP.
New Jersey

NIHIL OBSTAT: Rev. T. Kevin Corcoran, MA
Censor Librorum

IMPRIMATUR: ✠ Most Rev. David M. O'Connell, C.M., J.C.D., D.D.
Bishop of Trenton

January 6, 2021

The Nihil Obstat and Imprimatur are official declarations that a book or pamphlet is free of doctrinal or moral error. No implication is contained therein that those who have granted the Nihil Obstat and Imprimatur agree with the contents, opinions or statements expressed.

(T-946)

ISBN 978-1-953152-30-5

© 2021 by Catholic Book Publishing Corp.
Totowa, NJ 07512
Printed in Canada
catholicbookpublishing.com

Contents

Introduction

In 1962, Pope St. John XXIII added the name of St. Joseph to the Roman Canon, which is now the first Eucharistic Prayer used at Mass. In 2013, Pope Francis inserted St. Joseph's name into Eucharistic Prayers II, III, and IV. Now, at every celebration, immediately after naming the Blessed Virgin Mary, the priest mentions "Blessed Joseph, her spouse."

Some may not have realized that this is an addition. Others may simply think that adding a saint's name is a small matter. But, in light of the Church's faith, it was an extremely important change. Even more so since the Roman Canon had remained basically unaltered for 1362 years. The addition of St. Joseph to the Eucharistic Prayer is significant. *Lex orandi, lex credendi.* The way we pray reveals what we believe.

Our redemption is "the mystery of [God's] will…that he had predetermined in Christ to be realized when the fullness of time had been achieved" (Eph 1:9-10). At the Incarnation, when the fullness of time had come (Gal 4:4), God made that mystery known to Mary by an angel and to Joseph in a dream. He chose to work with them in a unique way to bring His only-begotten Son into the world. Mary and Joseph were the guardians of the mystery of our salvation in Christ from the very beginning.

The Incarnation and Redemption are one mystery: God redeeming us in Christ. The purpose for which the Son of God became man Jesus accomplishes by His suffering, death, and resurrection. He makes us sharers in the very life of God. This mystery of our redemption is celebrated and made present in its entirety in the Mass. For this reason, two Popes have directed Joseph to be mentioned in the Eucharistic Prayer. He belongs in the Mass, the memorial of our redemption, because he belongs to the very mystery of our redemption. Even before the apostles and martyrs, Joseph was given a most special place in the unfolding of God's plan for our salvation.

Along with Mary, Joseph plays a major role in receiving the Son of God into the human family. It is through Joseph that Jesus becomes the Son of David, bringing to fulfillment the prophecies about the coming of the Messiah. Joseph accepts this role because of his great faith.

Together with Mary, and in relation to Mary, he shares in this final phase of God's self-revelation in Christ and he does so from the very beginning. Looking at the gospel texts of both Matthew and Luke, one can also say that Joseph is the first to share in the faith of the Mother of God and that in doing so he supports his spouse in the faith of the divine annunciation. He is also the first to be placed by God on the path of Mary's "pilgrimage of faith." It is a path along which—especially at the time of Calvary and Pentecost—Mary will precede in a perfect way.

Pope St. John Paul II,
Redemptoris Custos, 5

As head of the Holy Family, Joseph cherished with constant care and sacrificial love both Mary and Jesus. He provided for their needs and protected them. He found a proper place for Jesus to be born in Bethlehem, to live in exile in Egypt, and to grow to manhood in Nazareth. He guarded the child Jesus from falling into the jealous hands of Herod, bent on killing Him. He kept Him safe within the arms of Mary. He guided Him as a wise and prudent father.

The house Joseph built was the home of Jesus who was to be the head of the Church. It was the home of the Virgin Mary who became the Mother of all the faithful. Joseph's home was the Church at its conception. And, just as he protected and cared for the Church in her beginning, so also, as Patron of the Universal Church, he looks on her as she extends her mission to the ends of the earth. All whom Jesus reckons His brothers and sisters and Mary loves as her own children, Joseph looks upon as members of his family to protect and guide. Thus, it is with great trust, we can turn to St. Joseph. With full confidence, we can pray to him for all our needs. He will never turn us away.

Because of the important role that St. Joseph has been given in the work of our redemption, Pope Francis established 2021 as a *Year in Honor of St. Joseph*. In the first millennium, the Church's understanding of Christ deepened through several Ecumenical Councils. In the following millennium, the Church's devotion to Mary increased, culminating with the infallible definition of her Immaculate Conception and her Assumption as well as the declaration of Mary as Mother of the Church. Moved by the strong desire to honor St. Joseph, Pope Francis with his Apostolic Letter *Patris Corde* initiated the third millennium as a time "to increase our love for this great saint...implore his intercession and to imitate his virtues and his zeal" (*Patris Corde*, 7).

The following biblical reflections are meant to open up the secret of Joseph's holiness. They serve as an introduction to praying to St. Joseph. All the saints in heaven stand before the throne of God, making constant intercession for us. "Some Saints are privileged to extend to us their patronage with particular efficacy in certain needs, but not in others; but our holy patron St. Joseph has the power to assist us in all cases, in every necessity, in every undertaking" (St. Thomas Aquinas).

First Day
Joseph the Husband of Mary

*"One who finds a wife finds happiness
and receives favor from the Lord."*

Prov 18:22

In the name of the Father, and the Son, and
the Holy Spirit.

℣. O God, come to my assistance.
℟. O Lord, make haste to help me.

O God, in Your divine providence You
were pleased to choose Blessed Joseph
to be the Spouse of the Immaculate Virgin
Mary and the Guardian of Your only-
begotten Son made man. In Your mercy,
You have given us St. Joseph as an example of holiness and a protector during our
earthly pilgrimage. By the grace of the Holy
Spirit, we pray, open our minds to understand the depth of Your love for us. Look
kindly on our prayer and, through the powerful intercession of St. Joseph, grant us all
the graces we need to follow Jesus as our
Lord and Savior who lives and reigns with
You in the unity of the Holy Spirit, one God,
forever and ever. Amen.

St. Joseph, pray for us.

JOSEPH appears for the first time in the New Testament at the end of Matthew's genealogy. Matthew opens his gospel by giving us Jesus' family tree. He wants to present Jesus to us as the Son of David, the long-awaited Messiah. Matthew begins the list of Jesus' royal ancestors by telling us that Abraham begot Isaac, Isaac begot Jacob and then continues using the same formula for each of the forty-one generations prior to Joseph. But when he comes to Joseph, Matthew breaks the pattern of begetting.

Matthew concludes his genealogy by simply naming "Joseph, the husband of Mary, who gave birth to Jesus who is called the Christ" (Mt 1:16). He does not tell us that Joseph begot Jesus. By changing the uninterrupted continuum of begetting, Matthew is affirming the Church's faith held from the beginning that Jesus was conceived not by power of man, but by the power of the Holy Spirit. In fact, in the verse immediately after the genealogy, Matthew makes this even more explicit. He says, "When [Jesus'] mother Mary was engaged to Joseph, but before they come to live together, she was found to be with child through the Holy Spirit" (Mt 1:18).

Nonetheless, while affirming the virginal conception of Jesus, Matthew presents Mary and Joseph as a married couple. He calls Joseph the husband of Mary (Mt 1:19) and Mary the wife of Joseph (Mt 1:20,24). Here is Scripture's first portrait of Joseph. He is the husband whom God chose for the mother of His only-begotten Son.

The Jews of the first century highly valued marriage. A Jewish man was expected to marry to fulfill the command of Genesis to increase and multiply (Gen 1:28). So important was marriage that a young man could put aside the study of the Torah to marry. In the first century, there was a passionate expectation of the imminent coming of the Messiah from among God's people. In this context, marriage took on almost a religious obligation. According to the custom of the day, men married at 18. They usually married younger women ready for marriage from age 13.

Religious iconography often portrays Joseph as a gray-haired man, advanced in years and much older than Mary. This image of Joseph already appears in the apocryphal second century *Protoevangelium of James* (9.2). A pious tradition held that Mary had taken a vow of virginity at a young age. Even such great saints as St. Gregory of Nyssa, St. Ambrose, and St. Augustine spoke of it.

However, there is no biblical evidence at all against the fact that Mary and Joseph married according to the custom of the time, intending to live a normal married life. This would all change with the Annunciation. But what did not change was the marriage of Joseph and Mary. They were true husband and wife, loving and caring for each other.

From the very first time Mary and Joseph are introduced as husband and wife, they appear together. They were united in heart and in affection. At the time of the Annunciation, they are an engaged couple looking forward to a happy marriage. In Nazareth, they shared a common life. They travel together to Joseph's ancestral home in Bethlehem for Jesus' birth. As a caring husband, Joseph protects Mary on the journey. When they arrive in Bethlehem, he finds them suitable lodgings. At the first hint of danger to their child, he takes Mary and Jesus to safety in Egypt.

Very telling of the good relationship Mary and Joseph have is Mary's statement when they find the boy Jesus in the Temple after searching for Him for three days. "Son, why have you done this to us? Your father and I have been searching for you with great anxiety" (Lk 2:48). Joseph was one with Mary in concern for the safety of Jesus. Mary's worry was Joseph's sorrow. Joseph was a sensitive husband who knew how to read the heart of his wife. And as a good spouse, he confronted the difficult situation, holding his wife's hand and reassuring her of his support.

In every good marriage, there is trust. When Gabriel announced that Mary was to bear Jesus, Joseph did not doubt her word. He certainly did not understand at first. But he trusted what she told him. He loved her so much he would do nothing to bring her harm. His trust was rewarded when God revealed to Joseph His will for him to take Mary as his wife.

As a good husband, Joseph believed in the goodness of his spouse. Their marriage was strong because they faced every challenge together. They trusted God completely. Like the marriage of Joseph and Mary, every good marriage grows in relationship to each spouse's commitment to God.

In Jewish tradition, a husband was not just to care and provide for his spouse. He was to love her. "Thus the sages laid down that a man shall honor his wife more than his own self and shall love her as he loves himself, and shall constantly seek to benefit her according to his means; that he shall not unduly impose his authority on her..." (Maim. Yad, Ishut 15:19–20). With perfect chastity, Joseph was the ideal husband who truly loved Mary more than himself. He was content to give her the honor due her as the Mother of the Lord.

St. Joseph was chosen among all men, to be the protector and guardian of the Virgin Mother of God; the defender and foster-father of the Infant-God, and the only co-operator upon earth, the one confidant of the secret of God in the work of the redemption of mankind.

St. Bernard of Clairvaux

CLOSING PRAYERS

Glorious Saint Joseph, spouse of the Immaculate Virgin, pray for me to have a pure, humble, charitable mind, and perfect resignation to the divine will. Be my guide, my father, and my model through life that I may die as you did in the arms of Jesus and Mary. Amen.

Prayer for a Special Intention

O Blessed St. Joseph, tenderhearted Father,
faithful guardian of Jesus, chaste spouse of
   the Mother of God,
I pray and beseech thee to offer to God the
   Father,
His Divine Son, bathed in Blood on the
   Cross for sinners,
and through the Holy Name of Jesus,
obtain for us from the Eternal Father, the
   favor I implore . . . Amen.

Memorare to St. Joseph

Remember, O most chaste spouse of the
Virgin Mary, that never was it known that
anyone who implored your help and sought
your intercession was left unassisted. Full
of confidence in your power I fly unto
you and beg your protection. Despise not
O Guardian of the Redeemer my humble
supplication, but in your bounty, hear and
answer me. Amen.

Our Father, Hail Mary, Glory be.

For additional prayers to St. Joseph see p. 87

Joseph the Father of Jesus

Second Day
Joseph the Father of Jesus

"As a father has compassion for his children, so the Lord has compassion on those who fear him."

Ps 103:13

In the name of the Father, and the Son, and the Holy Spirit.

℣. O God, come to my assistance.
℟. O Lord, make haste to help me.

O God, in your divine providence you were pleased to choose Blessed Joseph to be the Spouse of the Immaculate Virgin Mary and the Guardian of your only-begotten Son made man. In your mercy, you have given us St. Joseph as an example of holiness and a protector during our earthly pilgrimage. By the grace of the Holy Spirit, we pray, open our minds to understand the depth of your love for us. Look kindly on our prayer and, through the powerful intercession of St. Joseph, grant us all the graces we need to follow Jesus as our Lord and Savior who lives and reigns with you in the unity of the Holy Spirit, one God, forever and ever. Amen.

St. Joseph, pray for us.

IN THE proper development of every child, the attention, affection, encouragement, and unselfish love of both parents are invaluable. They provide the environment for the child to mature into a healthy and happy adult. They teach by their example. The vocation to be a mother and the vocation to be a father are complimentary and both necessary.

Mary was specially chosen by God to give flesh and blood to the only-begotten Son of God. She surrounded Jesus with love and affection as a caring mother. From the moment of His conception in her womb to the moment His crucified body was placed in the tomb, Mary was always united with Jesus. She never abandoned Him.

Joseph was also specially chosen by God. He was a true father to Jesus. "Fathers are not born, but made" (Pope Francis, *Patris Corde*, 7). A man does not become a father simply by bringing a child into the world, but by taking up the responsibility to care for that child. A man becomes a father only through sacrifice and love. By totally giving of himself, Joseph became the best father that walked the face of the earth.

Joseph provided for Jesus' physical needs and, together with Mary, created a home that was a haven of safety. The life of Jesus who was sent to save us depended on Joseph. Whether in Bethlehem, in Egypt, or in Nazareth, Joseph protected Jesus.

As Moses was protected from the threats of an evil Pharaoh by his own mother, Jesus was saved from the murderous intentions of a wicked king by Joseph His father. "In his relationship to Jesus, Joseph was the earthly shadow of the heavenly Father: he watched over him and protected him, never leaving him to go his own way. We can think of Moses' words to Israel: 'In the wilderness... you saw how the Lord your God carried you, just as one carries a child, all the way that you travelled' (Dt 1:31). In a similar way, Joseph acted as a father for his whole life" (Pope Francis, *Patris Corde*, 7).

Joseph was totally involved in the development and formation of Jesus. According to the Jewish custom in the first century, a father had the responsibility for the circumcision of his son, for ceremonial redemption of the firstborn son, for Torah study, and for teaching his son a trade. Joseph fulfilled these obligations with great love.

The home of Nazareth was a school of obedience. By always doing what God asked him to do, Joseph modeled for Jesus the proper response to the will of God. Four times an angel made known God's will to Joseph in a dream. Each time he declared his own "fiat," echoing the "fiat" of Mary at the Annunciation and preparing Jesus to utter His "fiat" beneath the shadows of Gethsemane.

As was the custom in his day, from the moment Jesus began to speak, Joseph began to teach Him the basics of Jewish belief (Deut 6:7). The obligation to study the Torah bound only men. Thus, Joseph was obliged to introduce Jesus to the study of the Scriptures. No doubt the deep love and knowledge of the Scriptures that characterized Jesus' public ministry were part of the inheritance He received from Joseph. Parents are the first and should always be the best teachers of their children in the ways of the faith. Certainly, Joseph was!

Jewish men living within 20 miles of Jerusalem were required to celebrate the Passover in the Holy City. Others would come at least once during their lifetime. Joseph took Mary and Jesus every year to Jerusalem for the feast. He was a man whose deep piety formed Jesus in the devout practice of religion.

When Jesus was twelve years old, He went to Jerusalem for the Passover with Mary and Joseph. When they discovered He had not joined the pilgrimage of family and friends back to Nazareth, they searched for Him in worry and anxiety. On finding Him in the Temple with the teachers of the law, Mary told Jesus, "Your father and I have been searching for you with great anxiety" (Lk 2:48). "Even the Virgin Mary, well aware that she has not conceived Christ as a result of conjugal relations with Joseph, still calls him Christ's father" (St Augustine, *Sermo* 51, 10, 16). Her words show the great respect she had for Joseph. Joseph was truly revered as the head of the family.

The patterns of behavior and interaction that we see in our parents during our childhood mold the way we instinctively respond to others in our adult years. In the respect and kindness, the tenderness and charity which Jesus spontaneously extended to all during His public ministry, we can detect Joseph's influence.

Joseph's deep reverence and affection for Mary, his constant concern for Jesus, and his hard work were the tools that God used to make Jesus in His human nature confident, outgoing, and willing to form good friendships. Joseph's generosity prepared the hands of Jesus to be open, gifting others with health and blessing.

According to the Babylonian Talmud, when a child experiences the taste of wheat (i.e., when he is weaned), he learns to say "abba," "dada," and "imma," "mama." Thus, from the moment Jesus began to speak, He addressed Joseph with the familiar word "abba" ("daddy"). He called to him with trust and confidence, not afraid but eager to be held and supported in his strong arms.

This single word "abba" exposes the heart of Jesus' own relationship to God. In His teaching, Jesus gives us the tender portrait of God as the Father who seeks the lost, welcomes back the prodigal and makes His love shine on both the just and the sinner. There is no doubt that, in Joseph who held Jesus' arms, training Him to walk and lifting Him up when He stumbled, Jesus first saw this tender reflection of His Father in heaven.

We should, indeed, honor St. Joseph, since the Son of God Himself was graciously pleased to honor him by calling him father. The Holy

Scriptures speak of him as the father of Jesus. "His father and mother were marveling at the things spoken—concerning Him" (Luke 2:33). Mary also used this name: "in sorrow thy father and I have been seeking thee" (Luke 2:48). If, then, the King of Kings was pleased to raise Joseph to so high a dignity, it is right and obligatory on our part to endeavor to honor him as much as we can.

St. Alphonse Liguori

CLOSING PRAYERS

Hail, Guardian of the Redeemer, Spouse of the Blessed Virgin Mary. To you God entrusted his only Son; in you Mary placed her trust; with you Christ became man. Blessed Joseph, to us too, show yourself a father and guide us in the path of life. Obtain for us grace, mercy and courage, and defend us from every evil. Amen.

Pope Francis

Prayer for a Special Intention

O Blessed St. Joseph, tenderhearted Father, faithful guardian of Jesus, chaste spouse of the Mother of God,

I pray and beseech thee to offer to God the Father,

His Divine Son, bathed in Blood on the Cross for sinners,

and through the Holy Name of Jesus,

obtain for us from the Eternal Father, the favor I implore . . . Amen.

Memorare to St. Joseph

Remember, O most chaste spouse of the Virgin Mary, that never was it known that anyone who implored your help and sought your intercession was left unassisted. Full of confidence in your power I fly unto you and beg your protection. Despise not O Guardian of the Redeemer my humble supplication, but in your bounty, hear and answer me. Amen.

Our Father, Hail Mary, Glory be.

For additional prayers to St. Joseph see p. 87

Third Day
Joseph the Just Man

*"The righteous is remembered
with blessings."*

Prov 10:7

In the name of the Father, and the Son, and
the Holy Spirit.

℣. O God, come to my assistance.
℟. O Lord, make haste to help me.

O God, in your divine providence you were
pleased to choose Blessed Joseph to be
the Spouse of the Immaculate Virgin Mary
and the Guardian of your only-begotten Son
made man. In your mercy, you have given
us St. Joseph as an example of holiness and
a protector during our earthly pilgrimage.
By the grace of the Holy Spirit, we pray,
open our minds to understand the depth of
your love for us. Look kindly on our prayer
and, through the powerful intercession of St.
Joseph, grant us all the graces we need to follow Jesus as our Lord and Savior who lives
and reigns with you in the unity of the Holy
Spirit, one God, forever and ever. Amen.

St. Joseph, pray for us.

OF ALL the people mentioned in Sacred Scripture, Joseph has the shortest biography. In narrating the birth of Jesus, Matthew describes Joseph with a single word. He tells us that Joseph was "a just man" (Mt 1:19). However, that one adjective "just" (righteous) unlocks for us the depth of Joseph's holiness. It places Joseph in the company of the great saints of the Old Testament who were likewise said to be just or upright. Calling Joseph just, Matthew places him at the end of a spiritual genealogy that includes Abel, Noah, Abraham, Josiah, Job, and John the Baptist.

In writing his gospel, Matthew favors the word "just" or "righteous." Whereas Mark who writes his gospel before Matthew uses the word only once, Matthew uses it seventeen times. When we call someone just, we are saying that they are fair in their judgments and that they give to each person what is their right. This is a very legalistic use of the word. It certainly applies to the owner in the parable of the laborers in the vineyard. The owner defrauds no worker of the wage they had agreed upon (Mt 20:4). Certainly this meaning is not absent in describing Joseph as just. But it does not say it all.

For Matthew, the word "just" is saturated with Old Testament meaning. It is derived from the Hebrew *sedeq*. This word denotes both a right standing before God and others and the right behavior that flows from being a member of the covenant community. In Matthew's gospel, "justice" or "righteousness" is a shorthand way to express God's plan to save His people through the covenant (Mt 3:15). It also expresses the people's response to God's saving action (Mt 5:20).

In terms of Old Testament piety, to be just means to be loyal, humble, gracious, merciful, and patient, as God is to His Chosen People. The just man is "generous in giving" (Ps 37:21) and "kind to others" (Wis 12:19). In fact, the prophet Ezekiel places all the virtues under the rubric of being just or righteous (Ezek 18:5-9). Thus, when Matthew calls Joseph "a just man," he is giving him the highest praise he can voice for his holiness. And rightly so.

Holiness is always more than obeying rules. It is the constant desire of the heart to do what is right in God's eyes. "Holiness... consists in accepting, with a smile, what Jesus sends us. It consists in accepting and following the will of God" (St. Teresa of Calcutta). Holiness makes us like God himself. We become self-giving, generous, willing to embrace hardship for others, as Joseph was.

Holiness is not being perfect. It is the road to perfection. It is the joyful response of gratitude to God for His goodness to us. It is the constant openness to God's grace to transform us.

When God calls us to a certain work or vocation, He gives us the grace to fulfill His plan. As St. Thomas Aquinas taught, God prepares us with many graces and with the gifts of nature necessary to fulfill our mission (*Summa Theologica*, III 98, 5 ad 3).Thus, when God called Joseph to care for Jesus and Mary, He gave him all the graces necessary to become holy.

God graced Joseph with the greatest of graces, because of his unique role in our redemption. "He is Holy Joseph, because according to the opinion of a great number of Doctors, he, as well as St. John Baptist, was sanctified even before he was born. He is Holy Joseph, because his office, of being spouse and protector of Mary, specially demanded sanctity. He is Holy Joseph, because no other Saint but he lived in such and so long intimacy and familiarity with the source of all holiness, Jesus, God incarnate, and Mary, the holiest of creatures" (St. John Henry Newman).

Saint Alphonse Liguori taught that Saint Joseph, like John the Baptist, was sanctified in his mother's womb prior to birth. In fact, some even speculate that, because of his unique place in God's plan, he never committed a deliberate sin. Other great theologians go as far as to say that there is no grace given to any other saint that was not given to Joseph and to Mary. "The Lord has arrayed Joseph, like with a sun, in all which the saints possess together in regard to light and splendor" (St. Gregory of Nazianzus).

Pope Benedict XVI has seen in the very first psalm a biblical portrait of Joseph. He once offered the following reflection.

St. Matthew describes St. Joseph with one word: he was a "just" man, "dikaios"...as we find it, for example, in Psalm 1; the man who is immersed in the word of God, who lives in the word of God and does not experience the Law as a "yoke" but rather as a "joy", who dwells in — we might say — the Law as a "Gospel". St Joseph was just, he was immersed in the word of God, written and transmitted through the wisdom of his people, and he was trained and called in this very way to know the Incarnate Word — the Word who came among us as a man — and was predestined to look after, to protect this Incarnate Word; this remained his mission for ever: to look after Holy Church and Our Lord.

Pope Benedict XVI, Address,
Redemptoris Mater Chapel, March 19, 2011

Closing Prayers

Prudent man,
who did not attach yourself to human securities
but was always open to respond to the unexpected
obtain for me the help of the divine spirit
so that I may also live in prudent detachment
of earthly securities.
Model of zeal, of constant work,
of silent faithfulness, of paternal kindness, obtain for me these blessings,
so that I may grow more in them every day,
and thus, day by day,
resemble Jesus, who is the model of full humanity.

Prayer for a Special Intention

O Blessed St. Joseph, tenderhearted Father,
faithful guardian of Jesus, chaste spouse
of the Mother of God,
I pray and beseech thee to offer to God the
Father,
His Divine Son, bathed in Blood on the
Cross for sinners,
and through the Holy Name of Jesus,
obtain for us from the Eternal Father, the
favor I implore . . . Amen.

Memorare to St. Joseph

Remember, O most chaste spouse of the
Virgin Mary, that never was it known that
anyone who implored your help and sought
your intercession was left unassisted. Full
of confidence in your power I fly unto
you and beg your protection. Despise not
O Guardian of the Redeemer my humble
supplication, but in your bounty, hear and
answer me. Amen.

Our Father, Hail Mary, Glory be.

For additional prayers to St. Joseph see p. 87

Joseph the Humble Man

Fourth Day
Joseph the Humble Man

"He guides the humble in what is right."

Ps 25:9

In the name of the Father, and the Son, and the Holy Spirit.

℣. O God, come to my assistance.
℟. O Lord, make haste to help me.

O God, in your divine providence you were pleased to choose Blessed Joseph to be the Spouse of the Immaculate Virgin Mary and the Guardian of your only-begotten Son made man. In your mercy, you have given us St. Joseph as an example of holiness and a protector during our earthly pilgrimage. By the grace of the Holy Spirit, we pray, open our minds to understand the depth of your love for us. Look kindly on our prayer and, through the powerful intercession of St. Joseph, grant us all the graces we need to follow Jesus as our Lord and Savior who lives and reigns with you in the unity of the Holy Spirit, one God, forever and ever. Amen.

St. Joseph, pray for us.

AT THE birth of Jesus, heaven and earth were joined together. No surprise, therefore, that angels played an important role in the Nativity. To the priest Zechariah offering incense in the Temple, the angel of the Lord appeared. The angel's first words to Zechariah, terrified and trembling at the sight of a heavenly messenger, were words of comfort: "Do not be afraid" (Lk 1:13). Then the angel informed him that he and his wife Elizabeth would have a son who would prepare the people for the ministry of Jesus.

The angel Gabriel appeared to Mary, a young girl in Nazareth. He announced that she would be the mother of Jesus, the long-expected Messiah. The angel assured her of God's favor. To Mary, who is troubled by this message, the angel says, "Do not be afraid…" (Lk 1:30).

The night when Jesus was born, an angel appeared to shepherds. They were startled as the night sky became resplendent with the glory of God. To these terrified shepherds, the angel repeats the same greeting. "Do not be afraid, for I bring you good news of great joy for all the people" (Lk 2:10).

The angel came to Zechariah. He came to Mary and to the shepherds. They beheld him with their eyes and were in awe. But to Joseph, the angel only appears in a dream. However, the angel also tells Joseph not to fear. The angel says, "Joseph, Son of David, do not be afraid to receive Mary into your home as your wife" (Mt 1:20). Although the birth of Jesus is a moment of great joy, it is an event enveloped in fear.

Sacred Scripture often speaks of fear. In fact, "do not be afraid" is the most frequent command in Scripture. It appears about 100 times in the Old Testament and about 40 times in the New Testament. In many instances, Sacred Scripture speaks of fear in a way much different than we do. It is when we unlock this biblical meaning of fear, we come to understand more deeply the reason why Joseph contemplates divorcing Mary when she is found with child.

Luke narrates Jesus' birth from the view of Mary. But Matthew records it from the perspective of Joseph. On the first page of his gospel, he introduces Mary as engaged to Joseph. According to the Jewish custom of their day, they were legally married. They are not yet living together as husband and wife when Mary is already with child. When Joseph becomes aware of this, "he resolved to divorce her quietly" (Mt 1:19).

Many read Matthew's account and come to the conclusion that Joseph does not know that Gabriel has announced to Mary that she is to conceive a child by the power of the Holy Spirit. Since he does know that the child is not his, he decides to divorce Mary privately. He loves her too much to shame her. In reality, divorcing Mary quietly would only delay public knowledge of her pregnancy before her marriage and the consequent shame.

It is highly improbable that Joseph entertained the suspicion that Mary was unfaithful. As the angel Gabriel himself said, Mary was "full of grace" (Lk 1:28). Mary's goodness was not something she could hide from others. No more could the sun's rays be kept hidden by the passing clouds than could Mary's virtues not touch those who knew her. Joseph knew Mary to be very holy. His engaged spouse was truly God-fearing. How could he doubt her innocence?

Furthermore, Mary herself was a most loving person. She was sensitive to the needs of others and filled with profound spiritual insight. Out of love for Joseph, she would hardly have left him lurking in the dark about the child in her womb.

In fact, the actual text of Matthew says, "When Mary was engaged to Joseph, but before they came to live together, she was found to be with child through the Holy Spirit" (Mt 1:18). This text certainly can mean that Mary had shared with her husband the astounding fact that her son was conceived by the power of the Holy Spirit. If Mary told Elizabeth, why would she not have discreetly told Joseph? He had more of a right to know this than Mary's aged relative.

Joseph's doubts are not about Mary. They are about himself. Mary is chosen by God. He does not know that he himself is also chosen. Awestruck, he does not presume that he is fit to live in close intimacy with Mary and the Son of God. Once God entered Mary's life in a singular way, Joseph feels unworthy of the role he had intended to have as her husband. He draws back in fear.

Joseph's fear is not the ordinary, natural human emotion we experience in face of danger. It is the Old Testament attitude of reverence, awe, or respect before the majesty of God. It is the biblical virtue that places us in the right relationship with God.

Thus, the psalmist says, "You who fear the Lord, praise him...give him glory. Revere him…" (Ps 22:24). According to St. Bernard, "Joseph wished to depart from [Mary] for the same reason that Peter kept away from our Lord, saying: 'Depart from me, O Lord, for I am a sinner;' for the same reason that the centurion kept him from his house, when he said, 'Lord, I am not worthy that you should come under my roof.'"

As a just man, holy in God's sight, Joseph draws back in fear, that is, in awe and reverence from the great mystery unfolding in Mary. But, once the angel appears to him in a dream and commands him to adopt Jesus as his son, Joseph accepts the special place God is giving him in His plan for our redemption. Joseph is truly humble. For fear of the Lord and humility are two faces of the same virtue (Prov 15:33; 22:4).

> *St. Joseph is the model of those humble ones that Christianity raises up to great destinies...he is the proof that in order to be a good and genuine follower of Christ, there is no need to do great things—it is enough to have the common, simple and human virtues, but they need to be true and authentic.*
>
> Pope St. John Paul II,
> *Redemptoris Custos*, 24

CLOSING PRAYERS

Faithful imitator of Jesus and Mary, humble Joseph, you who were as lowly in your eyes and in the opinion of men as you are great before God; teach me to be, like you, lowly and humble of heart. Alas, you know it, my sins, after having made me ungrateful to my God, have filled me again with a foolish pride, which is my soul's greatest wound. O kind Saint, my protector, my Patron and my Father, on this day I ask you for a virtue which is the foundation of all Christian perfection. Obtain for me humility, the grace to know myself and to despise me; obtain for me the grace to seek to please God alone in all my actions. May I, like you, love silence and the hidden life; may I, like you, be forgotten and despised by creatures; may the humiliations and the Cross of Jesus Christ be my share in this world, as they have been yours. O Jesus, Mary and Joseph, I now wish to put all my glory and my delights into humbling myself following your example. Amen.

The Monastery of the Magnificat,
Quebec, Canada

Prayer for a Special Intention

O Blessed St. Joseph, tenderhearted Father,
faithful guardian of Jesus, chaste spouse of
the Mother of God,
I pray and beseech thee to offer to God the
Father,
His Divine Son, bathed in Blood on the
Cross for sinners,
and through the Holy Name of Jesus,
obtain for us from the Eternal Father, the
favor I implore . . . Amen.

Memorare to St. Joseph

Remember, O most chaste spouse of the
Virgin Mary, that never was it known that
anyone who implored your help and sought
your intercession was left unassisted. Full
of confidence in your power I fly unto
you and beg your protection. Despise not
O Guardian of the Redeemer my humble
supplication, but in your bounty, hear and
answer me. Amen.

Our Father, Hail Mary, Glory be.

For additional prayers to St. Joseph see p. 87

Fifth Day
Joseph the Man of Trust

"Blessed are those who trust in the Lord and whose hope is the Lord."

Jer 17:7

In the name of the Father, and the Son, and the Holy Spirit.

℣. O God, come to my assistance.
℟. O Lord, make haste to help me.

O God, in your divine providence you were pleased to choose Blessed Joseph to be the Spouse of the Immaculate Virgin Mary and the Guardian of your only-begotten Son made man. In your mercy, you have given us St. Joseph as an example of holiness and a protector during our earthly pilgrimage. By the grace of the Holy Spirit, we pray, open our minds to understand the depth of your love for us. Look kindly on our prayer and, through the powerful intercession of St. Joseph, grant us all the graces we need to follow Jesus as our Lord and Savior who lives and reigns with you in the unity of the Holy Spirit, one God, forever and ever. Amen.

St. Joseph, pray for us.

SACRED Scripture often speaks of fear. It mentions fear over 300 times. However, Sacred Scripture speaks of fear in two different ways. In some places, it has the deeply spiritual meaning of reverence or awe. In other places, it simply is the natural emotion we experience when facing something beyond our power or understanding. We instinctively feel afraid.

In itself, fear is not something bad. It is nature's way of protecting us. In the face of danger, it makes us more cautious. In the face of difficult situations, it makes us more prudent.

Thus, when the Hebrews are fleeing Egypt, they suddenly catch sight of Pharaoh's army. The Red Sea is in front of them. The Egyptians in fast pursuit behind them. And they become terrified. Moses tells them, "Do not be afraid. Be strong, and you will see the salvation that the Lord will work for you today,…The Lord will battle for you. Be calm!" (Ex 14:13-14).

Many times, Scripture speaks of fear in this way. It is the panic or terror that takes hold of us in the face of danger. Thus, for example, the prophet Elijah experiences great fear. He has just pronounced a death sentence against king Ahaziah. When one of Ahaziah's captains come to bring him to the king, Elijah is terrified. Then, "the angel of the Lord said to Elijah, 'Go down with him and do not be afraid of him'" (2 Ki 1:15). Jesus himself speaks of this same type of fear that grips us in times of persecution. He says, "I tell you, my friends, have no fear of those who kill the body and after that can do nothing further" (Lk 12:4).

Joseph, the guardian of Mary and Jesus, was thoroughly human. He experienced this type of fear. When Herod was about to dispatch his soldiers to kill the child Jesus, an angel appeared to Joseph and told him to take Jesus and Mary to Egypt for safety. Most certainly, Joseph made that journey with some fear and trepidation. Any moment, the soldiers of Herod could overtake him. But his fear was mitigated by the fact that the angel of the Lord already gave him the way to escape danger (Mt 2:13-15). But it is otherwise when he returns to the land of Israel.

After Herod dies, the angel comes to Joseph again in a dream and instructs him to take the child and his mother back to the land of Israel. Joseph obeys and begins the journey back to Bethlehem. He trusts the word of the Lord. But, as he approaches the land of Judah, he discovers that Archelaus has succeeded his father Herod. Like his dreaded father, he was well known for his cruelty.

Almost immediately on coming to power, Archelaus had 3,000 people executed in the Temple during Passover. He was so cruel that the Jews and Samaritans united in an appeal to Rome against him. Within nine years of mounting the throne, Augustus removed him and banished him to Vienne in Gaul.

Archelaus had deposed three high priests during his short reign. He would have thought nothing of killing a child hailed as the long-awaited Messiah. "Learning that Archelaus had succeeded his father Herod in Judea, he was afraid to go there" (Mt 2:22). Instead, the Holy Family goes to Galilee, to the small town of Nazareth.

Joseph experienced the very human emotion of fear. The angel had only given him the command to return to Israel. God had not given him detailed instructions about his reentry into the Promised Land. God trusted Joseph to use his reason to choose the most suitable place to raise his family. God does not dictate to any one of us every single choice we have to make. He gives intellect and will and the freedom to use them as best we can.

Facing the imminent threat of the danger that Archelaus was to the child, Joseph chose not to let fear paralyze his steps. His trust in God's providence was the antidote to his fear. He had ample assurance of God's care for him and his family. Most assuredly, he remembered the words spoken to Joshua as he was leading God's family back into the land of Abraham, Isaac, and Jacob after their time in Egypt. "Be strong and brave, do not be afraid nor dismayed. I, the Lord, your God will be with you wherever you go" (Jos 1:9).

It is the sure faith in the goodness of God that overcomes fear and begets hope. God used the fear of Joseph to bring the Holy Family to Nazareth. God uses all the circumstances of our lives, even those that leave us searching in the dark, to guide us to accomplish His purpose. We need only be like Joseph, humble enough to change our plans and trust in God's providence.

Let us turn with holy confidence to the glorious St. Joseph, let us present to him our spiritual and temporal needs and not fear even for an instant that he might exercise his patronage weakly. Will he, the great Saint whom Jesus and Mary obeyed, who provided Jesus and Mary with their daily bread, be invoked in vain? No: not without a profound mystery of mercy, in this century the figure of the glorious Patriarch stands out and shines with new light...

St. Luigi Guanella

CLOSING PRAYERS

Blessed Saint Joseph,
your intercession can make possible impossible things.
Come to help me in these moments of anguish and hardship.
Take under your protection the difficult and grave situations I commend to you,
so they have a happy solution according to God's will.
My beloved father,
I trust you entirely
and abandon myself as a small child

sleeping in his dad's arms. That could not be
said I appealed to you in vain.

And as you, through the Lord,

can everything accomplish in front of Jesus
and Mary,

show me your kindness is as great as your
power. Amen.

Prayer for a Special Intention

Blessed St. Joseph, tenderhearted Father,

faithful guardian of Jesus, chaste spouse of
the Mother of God,

I pray and beseech thee to offer to God the
Father,

His Divine Son, bathed in Blood on the
Cross for sinners,

and through the Holy Name of Jesus,

obtain for us from the Eternal Father, the
favor I implore . . . Amen.

Memorare to St. Joseph

Remember, O most chaste spouse of the
Virgin Mary, that never was it known that
anyone who implored your help and sought
your intercession was left unassisted. Full
of confidence in your power I fly unto
you and beg your protection. Despise not
O Guardian of the Redeemer my humble

supplication, but in your bounty, hear and answer me. Amen.

Our Father, Hail Mary, Glory be.

For additional prayers to St. Joseph see p. 87

Sixth Day
Joseph the Man of Silence

"In God alone is my soul at rest."

Ps 62:2

In the name of the Father, and the Son, and the Holy Spirit.

℣. O God, come to my assistance.
℟. O Lord, make haste to help me.

O God, in your divine providence you were pleased to choose Blessed Joseph to be the Spouse of the Immaculate Virgin Mary and the Guardian of your only-begotten Son made man. In your mercy, you have given us St. Joseph as an example of holiness and a protector during our earthly pilgrimage. By the grace of the Holy Spirit, we pray, open our minds to understand the depth of your love for us. Look kindly on our prayer and, through the powerful intercession of St. Joseph, grant us all the graces we need to follow Jesus as our Lord and Savior who lives and reigns with you in the unity of the Holy Spirit, one God, forever and ever. Amen.

St. Joseph, pray for us.

IN THE Gospel of Luke, the angel Gabriel announces the birth of Jesus to Mary. She responds first with a question (Lk 1:34) and then with a joyful, resounding *fiat* to God's will (Lk 1:38). When Elizabeth praises Mary for her belief in what the angel told her, Mary turns her gaze heavenward, extolling God in the poetry of the *Magnificat* (Lk 1:46-55). Then, when Mary and Joseph find Jesus in the Temple, Mary speaks for the last time in the Gospel of Luke (Lk 2:48).

In Mark and Matthew, Mary says not a single word. However, in the Gospel of John, Mary speaks twice. At the marriage feast of Cana, she discreetly asks Jesus to work His first miracle (Jn 2:3) and then tells the waiters to follow His instructions (Jn 2:5). After this incident, she only appears at the foot of the Cross in the fourth gospel. Jesus speaks to her, but she remains silent and sorrowing.

Mary's words are few but rich in meaning. She is the first to hear the gospel and accept it. Mary is the first and best disciple. Her words reveal her deep spirituality as one of the *anawim*. She belongs to that group of faithful Jews who depend totally on God.

Closest to Mary in the mystery of our redemption is Joseph. He is the greatest saint after the Mother of God. Yet, amazingly, from Joseph, we hear not a single word in any of the four gospels. In the Gospel of Matthew, an angel appears to Joseph four times, informing him of God's will. Joseph listens, but says nothing.

Zechariah sings the *Benedictus*. Simeon utters his *Nunc Dimittis*. But no song of joy is heard from the lips of Joseph. He lives in the closest of intimacies with Mary and Jesus. Yet there is not recorded a single tender word to either. In the entire New Testament, Joseph is silent.

In the wisdom of God, the silence of Joseph provides the secret to receiving the Word and living it in our lives. As the Book of Wisdom reminds us, "When a profound silence encompassed all things and the night was at midpoint in its swift course, [God's] all-powerful Word leapt from [God's] royal throne in heaven" (Wis 18:14-15). The Word made His dwelling among us when all was in peaceful silence. God comes to us not in the roar of thunder but in the quiet whisper of the wind (1 Ki 19:11-13). He comes most easily to us not in a multitude of words, but in silence.

There can be no relationship with God without silence. There can be no genuine encounter with God without it. Joseph's silence was the result of his deep encounter with the Lord. With his silence, he surrounded Jesus and Mary with a calm that this world cannot give. It was the peace that rose spontaneously from his deeper personal prayer.

All prayer is communication with God. And the alpha and omega of all prayer is silence. Silence at the beginning of prayer is a prayer itself. It expresses the words Eli the priest put on the lips of the young boy Samuel. At a time "when the word of the Lord was rare" (1 Sam 3:1), Eli told Samuel to say, "Speak Lord for your servant is listening" (1 Sam 3:9). The silence of Joseph was his receptivity to God. That is why each time the angel commands him to do something, he immediately executes the command without an objection.

Prayer is not a matter of simply uttering a petition or exclaiming praise of God. It is about communicating with God. Prayer is the road that leads to communion with God. When we come to the end of that road, we stand face to face with the mystery of God. In the presence of God, words fail and there is silence. The ultimate end of all prayer is our loving gaze on the face of God. Wordless. Speechless. Filled with awe beyond all telling.

The silence of Joseph made him conscious of the divine mystery that was directing his life. It is "a silence that reveals in a special way the inner portrait of the man. The Gospels speak exclusively of what Joseph 'did.' Still, they allow us to discover in his 'actions'—shrouded in silence as they are— an aura of deep contemplation. Joseph was in daily contact with the mystery 'hidden from ages past,' and which 'dwelt' under his roof" (Pope St. John Paul II, *Redemptoris Custos*, 25).

For Jesus, His home of Nazareth was a school of contemplation. Mary who pondered all things in her heart (Lk 2:19) and Joseph who kept silent were His pedagogues. He learned from them the importance of silence.

Jesus withdrew often during His public ministry to be silent and alone with the Father (Lk 5:16). His solitude and stillness in prayer opened Him in His humanity to the compassion, mercy, and wisdom of heaven itself. Because He valued silence so much, in the midst of His busy ministry, Jesus urged His disciples to follow His example, saying "Come away with me, by yourselves, to a deserted place and rest for a while"(Mk 6:31). The silence of Joseph was an inheritance that Jesus desired to share with His new family of disciples, then and now.

His is a silence permeated by contemplation of the mystery of God, in an attitude of total availability to His divine wishes. In other words, the silence of St. Joseph was not the sign of an inner void, but on the contrary, of the fullness of faith he carried in his heart, and which guided each and every one of his thoughts and actions.

Pope Benedict XVI, Angelus, December 18, 2005

CLOSING PRAYERS

Fortify me with the grace of your Holy Spirit and give your peace to my soul that I may be free of all needless anxiety, solicitude and worry. Help me to desire always that which is pleasing and acceptable to you so that your will may be my will.

St. Frances Xavier Cabrini

Prayer for a Special Intention

O Blessed St. Joseph, tenderhearted Father,
faithful guardian of Jesus, chaste spouse of
the Mother of God,
I pray and beseech thee to offer to God the
Father,
His Divine Son, bathed in Blood on the
Cross for sinners,
and through the Holy Name of Jesus,
obtain for us from the Eternal Father, the
favor I implore . . . Amen.

Memorare to St. Joseph

Remember, O most chaste spouse of the
Virgin Mary, that never was it known that
anyone who implored your help and sought
your intercession was left unassisted. Full
of confidence in your power I fly unto
you and beg your protection. Despise not
O Guardian of the Redeemer my humble
supplication, but in your bounty, hear and
answer me. Amen.

Our Father, Hail Mary, Glory be.

For additional prayers to St. Joseph see p. 87

Joseph the Worker

"If you see a man who is skilled in his work, remember that he will serve kings."

Prov 22:29

In the name of the Father, and the Son, and the Holy Spirit.

℣. O God, come to my assistance.
℟. O Lord, make haste to help me.

O God, in your divine providence you were pleased to choose Blessed Joseph to be the Spouse of the Immaculate Virgin Mary and the Guardian of your only-begotten Son made man. In your mercy, you have given us St. Joseph as an example of holiness and a protector during our earthly pilgrimage. By the grace of the Holy Spirit, we pray, open our minds to understand the depth of your love for us. Look kindly on our prayer and, through the powerful intercession of St. Joseph, grant us all the graces we need to follow Jesus as our Lord and Savior who lives and reigns with you in the unity of the Holy Spirit, one God, forever and ever. Amen.

St. Joseph, pray for us.

THE LOUVRE Museum in Paris houses the evocative 17th century oil painting of *Joseph the Carpenter* by Georges de La Tour. The artist shows a young Jesus holding a candle to give light to Joseph hard at work drilling a piece of wood with an auger. Pieces of wood on the ground of the carpenter shop resemble a cross. They foreshadow the sacrifice by which Jesus establishes the kingdom of God in this world. The artist beautifully captures the importance of Jesus' upbringing. Joseph is preparing Jesus for His work in building up the kingdom of God on this earth.

Every Jewish father had to teach his son a trade or instruct him in a profession so that he lived an honorable life (Babylonian Talmud, *Kiddushin* 29a). Joseph passed on his profession to Jesus. In Matthew's gospel, the people in Nazareth are astonished when Jesus teaches in their synagogue. They wonder from where came His great wisdom. They scoff at Him, saying, "Is this not the carpenter's son?" (Mt 13:55). In this same event in Mark's gospel, the people directly refer to Jesus Himself as "the carpenter, the son of Mary" (Mk 6:3). Both Jesus and His father Joseph were, therefore, well known in Nazareth as sharing the same profession.

In the early apocryphal literature such as the *Gospel of Thomas* and the *Syriac-Arabic Infancy Gospel*, popular imagination embellished the gospel facts. Joseph is depicted as a carpenter who makes tools such as plows and yokes for farmers and tables and beds for families. They limit Joseph to be a woodworker. But the one word that the gospels use for Joseph's work enlarges our vision of the kind of work Joseph did.

The gospels use the Greek word τέκτων (tekton) to describe Joseph's occupation. Translations render this as "carpenter." While this is not wrong, it is not an accurate translation. The word is better translated as "craftsman" or "builder." It designates someone who works not only in wood, but in stone or even in iron.

Stone was plentiful in Nazareth and throughout the land. Trees were scarce. If Joseph only worked in wood, he would have had a very difficult time earning a living. Since the houses and buildings in Nazareth and the surrounding areas were made of stone, it is no stretch of the imagination to picture Joseph chiseling and carving stone, stacking building blocks and making walls, fences, and houses. Since the Jews throughout Galilee used stoneware because of ritual purity, he would have also carved stone storage jars and tableware.

Even though Nazareth was a small village, there would have been plenty of work for a stonemason or builder like Joseph and his son Jesus. Nearby was Sepphoris. Herod Antipas was building it up as his capital in Galilee. His massive building projects were making this city set on a hill "the jewel of all Galilee" (Flavius Josephus, *Ant.* 18.27). During Jesus' youth, skilled and expert workers from the area were enlisted in developing this metropolis just three miles from His humble home. In fact, within walking distance of Nazareth and Sepphoris, there were stone quarries where Jesus could have watched His father chisel and select the best building blocks to use in construction of Herod's new capital.

Joseph knew what it was to work hard. With the sweat of his brow and the strength of his arm, he provided food, shelter, clothing, and some earthly pleasures to Mary and Jesus. His call to be the protector of the Holy Family, far from insulating him from the hardships of life, made him strong and generous in undertaking them with joy.

The gospels give only a brief, passing notice of Joseph's work. But their record of his work has permanent value. For Joseph the worker gave great dignity to human labor. He showed that the physical world and the things of this earth have a place in God's plan for our redemption.

"Human work, and especially manual labor, receive special prominence in the Gospel. Along with the humanity of the Son of God, work too has been taken up in the mystery of the Incarnation, and has also been redeemed in a special way. At the work-bench where he plied his trade together with Jesus, Joseph brought human work closer to the mystery of the Redemption" (Pope St. John Paul II, *Redemptoris Custos,* 22).

From His experience working with His father, Jesus not only learned a trade but He also collected the building blocks to construct some of His most memorable teachings. Jesus never speaks of wood carpentry, but He does talk about masonry. In speaking His parables He talks about digging a wine-press and building a tower in a vineyard to protect it (Mt 21:33). He offers the wisdom of building a house not on sand, but on the solid foundation of rock (Mt 7:24-27).

When Jesus decides to build His Church, He does so on the Rock who is Peter (Mt 16:18). Images of construction haunt the teaching of Jesus. In fact, at the end of His ministry, in speaking to His adversaries, Jesus predicts His own Death and Resurrection, saying, "The stone that the builders rejected has become the cornerstone; by the Lord has this been done, and it is wonderful in our eyes" (Mt 21:42).

In those hidden years of Jesus' life in Nazareth, something even more profound was taking place in Joseph's workshop. The people of Galilee, unlike their counterparts in Judea, staunchly resisted any influence of paganism to creep its way into their tightly-knit religious community. They were fiercely devoted to their faith. They spent hours studying and memorizing the Torah. No doubt Joseph not only passed on his trade to Jesus, but he lightened the hours of hard labor with repeating the words of Sacred Scripture. Joseph was not only carving and fashioning stone, he was laying the foundation for Jesus' vast knowledge of Scripture. How inestimable his work!

Joseph, of royal blood, united by marriage to the greatest and holiest of women, reputed father of the Son of God, passed his life in labor, and won by the toil of the artisan the needful support of his family. It is, then, true that the condition of the lowly has nothing shameful in it, and the work of the laborer is not only not dishonoring, but can, if virtue be joined to it, be singularly ennobled. Joseph, content with his slight possessions, bore the trials consequent on a fortune so slender, with greatness of soul, in imitation of his Son, who having put on the form of a slave, being the Lord of life, subjected himself of his own free will to the spoliation and loss of everything.

Pope Leo XIII, *Quamquam Pluries*, 4

CLOSING PRAYERS

O Glorious St Joseph, model of all who are devoted to labor, obtain for me the grace to work in the spirit of penance in expiation of my many sins; to work conscientiously by placing love of duty above my inclinations; to gratefully and joyously deem it an honor to employ and to develop by labor the gifts I have received from God, to work methodically, peacefully, and in moderation and patience, without ever shrinking from it through weariness or difficulty to work above all, with purity of intention and unselfishness, having unceasingly before my eyes death and the account I have to render of time lost, talents unused, good not done, and vain complacency in success, so baneful to the work of God. All for Jesus, all for Mary, all to imitate thee, O Patriarch St. Joseph! This shall be my motto for life and eternity. Amen.

Pope St. Pius X

Prayer for a Special Intention

O Blessed St. Joseph, tenderhearted Father, faithful guardian of Jesus, chaste spouse of
    the Mother of God,
 I pray and beseech thee to offer to God the
    Father,
His Divine Son, bathed in Blood on the
    Cross for sinners,
and through the Holy Name of Jesus,
obtain for us from the Eternal Father, the
    favor I implore . . . Amen.

Memorare to St. Joseph

Remember, O most chaste spouse of the Virgin Mary, that never was it known that anyone who implored your help and sought your intercession was left unassisted. Full of confidence in your power I fly unto you and beg your protection. Despise not O Guardian of the Redeemer my humble supplication, but in your bounty, hear and answer me. Amen.

Our Father, Hail Mary, Glory be.

For additional prayers to St. Joseph see p. 87

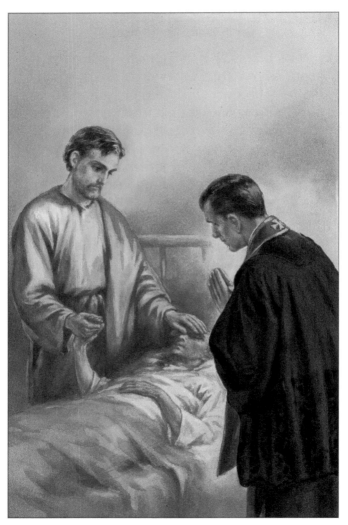

Joseph the Patron of a Happy Death

Eighth Day

Joseph the Patron of a Happy Death

8

"Precious in the eyes of the Lord is the death of his faithful ones."

Ps 116:15

In the name of the Father, and the Son, and the Holy Spirit.

℣. O God, come to my assistance.
℟. O Lord, make haste to help me.

O God, in your divine providence you were pleased to choose Blessed Joseph to be the Spouse of the Immaculate Virgin Mary and the Guardian of your only-begotten Son made man. In your mercy, you have given us St. Joseph as an example of holiness and a protector during our earthly pilgrimage. By the grace of the Holy Spirit, we pray, open our minds to understand the depth of your love for us. Look kindly on our prayer and, through the powerful intercession of St. Joseph, grant us all the graces we need to follow Jesus as our Lord and Savior who lives and reigns with you in the unity of the Holy Spirit, one God, forever and ever. Amen.

St. Joseph, pray for us.

IN 1751, Thomas Gray published his poem *Elegy Written in a Country Churchyard*. It instantly became popular. Today it is considered one of the best-known poems in the English language. The poem's masterful and musical use of the English brings into the light the dark reality of death that all must face. In the following lines, he expresses the universality of death.

> The boast of heraldry, the pomp of
>   power,
> And all that beauty, all that wealth
>   e'er gave,
> Awaits alike the inevitable hour.
> The paths of glory lead but to the
>   grave.

The sufferings we endure in life are many and varied. Some may escape poverty; others, depression. Chronic illness does not strike everyone. But no one escapes death. As Ecclesiastes teaches, "the worst evil of all the things that happen under the sun is this: that the same fate befalls everyone…they descend to the dead" (Eccl 9:3).

Death is the sad inheritance that Adam and Eve left all their children. As St. Paul teaches, "Sin entered the world as the result of one man, and death as a result of sin, and thus death has afflicted the entire human race inasmuch as everyone has sinned" (Rom 5:12). With the advances of science and medicine, the average life span is increasing. But nothing can halt the arrival of death. Whether it comes when we are in our youthful vigor or in our declining years, its arrival is certain. Sudden or slow, death gains entry to our home.

With painful accuracy, the gospels record the suffering and death of Jesus on the Cross. But of the death of His parents there is not a word. As Jesus hung dying on Golgotha, Mary stood there. The sword that Simeon had promised at the Presentation of the child Jesus in the Temple was piercing her maternal heart. Mary stands alone, no brother, no sister of Jesus to console her. Her beloved Joseph no longer with her.

Throughout Jesus' public ministry, Mary accompanied Him. From Cana to Calvary, she never abandoned Him. Joseph is mentioned in the narratives of Jesus' infancy but never during the public ministry of Jesus. Tradition holds that Joseph died before Jesus began preaching the kingdom of God. Most certainly, if he were alive, he would have accompanied Mary in following Jesus.

And, there is no doubt that, when Jesus was dying on the Cross, He would not have entrusted His widowed mother to John the Beloved disciple if Joseph were still alive.

From the very beginning, the Church has held sacred the memory of Joseph. He is an essential player in the drama of our redemption. The gospels preserve his God-given mission in the upbringing of Jesus. However, as if with deliberate humility, Joseph quietly slips from our view once Jesus begins His public ministry. He would let nothing detract from Jesus' preaching about His Father in heaven.

Apocryphal gospels have tried to fill in the information we lack about Joseph. For instance, the 6th century *History of Joseph the Carpenter*, written in Egypt, gives a lengthy description of Joseph at the age of 111 dying a peaceful death with Mary, Jesus, and the angels at his side. As inspiring as this account may be, it is pure imagination.

Joseph died. Mary and Jesus were alive. These are the bare facts unadorned by pious musings. So strong and tender was the love of the Holy Family that Mary remained united with Jesus even on Golgotha. It would be impossible to entertain the thought that Mary and Jesus abandoned Joseph in his final hour.

Jesus respected Joseph very much. After the finding of Jesus in the Temple, Jesus returned to Nazareth, and "was obedient to them" (Lk 2:51). All the sacrifices Joseph selflessly made for Jesus and Mary only increased Jesus' devotion to Joseph. Whatever the circumstance, filial love, coupled with compassion for His own mother, brought Jesus to Joseph's death bed.

Jesus came to conquer death itself. Moved by the pleas of Jairus for his daughter, he brought her back to life. Touched by the sorrow of the widow of Nain, he restored her dead son to his mother. Standing at the grave of his beloved friend Lazarus, He summoned him forth to life. But only after He had shed tears of great sorrow. How could His human heart not be saddened with grief as He lost His own dear father, closer to Him than any friend! How many tears must He have mingled with those of Mary as together they watched Joseph leave this world!

Grief and sadness were not strangers to the Holy Family. But neither were peace and joy at the moment of death. Joseph's life ends where Jesus' public ministry begins.

His mission is complete. He has done the will of the Father in heaven. "He was chosen by the eternal Father as the trustworthy guardian and protector of His greatest treasures, namely, His divine Son and Mary, Joseph's wife. He carried out this vocation with complete fidelity until at last God called him, saying, 'Good and faithful servant, enter into the joy of your Lord'" (St. Bernardine of Siena).

With a sense of accomplishment, Joseph gracefully lets fall from his hands the tools of his trade. Surrounded by the love of Mary and Jesus, he slips from their hands to rest in the bosom of Abraham. In time, Joseph had been privileged to gaze each day with tender devotion on the face of Jesus, "the reflection of God's glory and the perfect expression of his being" (Heb 1:3). He now passes into the eternal light of heaven, there with rapturous joy to see God face to face.

The death of Joseph is less a departure from life and more of a coming into the fullness of life. It is the peaceful crowning of the life of a truly just man. Neither the most skilled writer nor the most talented artist could ever have captured this moment of divine grace.

A saint, who had so loved in life, could only die of love; for his soul could not love Jesus enough amidst the distractions of this life; and having fulfilled the duty required of him in tending the childhood of his Lord, what remained but that he should say to the Eternal Father, "I have finished the work which You gave me to do" (Jn 17:4): and to the Son, "O my child, as your heavenly Father placed your Body in my hands on the day when you came into the world, so now, in this day of my departure from the world, I place my soul in yours." Such, I conceive, was the death of this great Patriarch.

St. Francis de Sales

CLOSING PRAYERS

O great St. Joseph, obtain for me from Jesus the grace to keep all God's commandments, and to promptly obey the secret calls and inspirations of Heaven.

St. Joseph, obtain for me the grace to do all my actions to please God alone.

O St. Joseph, ask of Jesus, for me, the grace never to commit a mortal sin.

O my dear St. Joseph, watch over me during life, be with me at death, and obtain for me Paradise.

St. Joseph, spouse of Mary, beg of the Blessed Virgin to obtain for me, from Jesus her Son, the grace to lead a holy life and die a happy death.

O glorious St. Joseph, the model, the patron, and the comforter of the dying, I now beg thy protection at the last moment of my life; obtain, I beseech thee, that I may die the death of the just. Amen.

Prayer for a Special Intention

O Blessed St. Joseph, tenderhearted Father, faithful guardian of Jesus, chaste spouse of
    the Mother of God,
I pray and beseech thee to offer to God the
    Father,
His Divine Son, bathed in Blood on the
    Cross for sinners,
and through the Holy Name of Jesus,
    obtain for us from the Eternal Father,
    the favor I implore . . . Amen.

Memorare to St. Joseph

Remember, O most chaste spouse of the Virgin Mary, that never was it known that anyone who implored your help and sought your intercession was left unassisted. Full of confidence in your power I fly unto you and beg your protection. Despise not O Guardian of the Redeemer my humble supplication, but in your bounty, hear and answer me. Amen.

Our Father, Hail Mary, Glory be.

For additional prayers to St. Joseph see p. 87

*Joseph Patron of Families and
the Universal Church*

Ninth Day

Joseph Patron of Families and the Universal Church

9

"He appointed him master of his house-hold and as ruler of all his possessions."
(Ps 105:21)

In the name of the Father, and the Son, and the Holy Spirit.

℣. O God, come to my assistance.
℟. O Lord, make haste to help me.

O God, in your divine providence you were pleased to choose Blessed Joseph to be the Spouse of the Immaculate Virgin Mary and the Guardian of your only-begotten Son made man. In your mercy, you have given us St. Joseph as an example of holiness and a protector during our earthly pilgrimage. By the grace of the Holy Spirit, we pray, open our minds to understand the depth of your love for us. Look kindly on our prayer and, through the powerful intercession of St. Joseph, grant us all the graces we need to follow Jesus as our Lord and Savior who lives and reigns with you in the unity of the Holy Spirit, one God, forever and ever. Amen.

St. Joseph, pray for us.

79

AT MIDDAY on the road to Damascus, with a light brighter than the sun, Paul had a vision of Christ. The Risen Lord appeared to him, appointing him the Apostle to the Gentiles (Acts 9:3-8; 22:6-11; 26:13-19). At noon on the rooftop of Simon the tanner's house in Joppa, Peter had a vision telling him to baptize Cornelius, the first Gentile (Acts 10:9-16). Cornelius himself on the previous day had an afternoon vision telling him to send for Peter (Acts 10:1-8). And Paul one night was told in a vision to go to Macedonia, thus bringing the faith from Asia into Europe (Acts 16:9-10). But, in the entire New Testament, only Joseph receives his role in our redemption in dreams shrouded in the silence of the night.

In the New Testament, Joseph of Nazareth uniquely resembles the patriarch Joseph in the Old Testament. God communicates His saving plan to both in dreams. Both have a similar role in protecting God's chosen ones. Each of them clearly understands God's communication to them in dreams; and, they cooperate with His will.

In the Old Testament, the patriarch Joseph learns in a dream that God plans to set him over his brothers to save their lives (Gen 37:5-9;

Gen 42:6-9). Joseph is taken into Egypt as a prisoner. However, when his virtue is seen, Joseph becomes manager of Potiphar's house (Gen 39:4), then keeper of the prison (Gen 39:22), and finally Master of Pharaoh's house and Lord of all the land of Egypt (Gen 41: 40-45). Through these events of history, God placed Joseph in the position where he could save the family of Jacob from death (Gen 45:4-8).

In many ways, Joseph in the Old Testament foreshadows the Joseph in the New Testament. Like him, Joseph in Matthew's gospel learns in a dream God's plan for him. He is to be the husband of Mary and father of Jesus. He is chosen by God to be the guardian and protector of the Holy Family (Mt 1:20; 2:13, 19-22). The patriarch Joseph saved the lives of his family by going down into Egypt. Joseph of Nazareth saved the life of Jesus. He flees to Egypt to escape the murderous threats of Herod the Great; and, then, on return, he settles in Nazareth to avoid the evil Archelaus.

The patriarch Joseph provided grain for his family in time of a severe famine. Joseph of Nazareth never let his family suffer want. Pharaoh appointed Joseph "master of his

household and ruler of all his possessions"
(Ps 105:21). God made Joseph head of the
house of Nazareth. Even God's own Son was
subject to his authority (Lk 2:51).

With the same protection that Joseph surrounded Jesus, he guarded the dignity and
honor of Mary. He did not divorce her when
she was with child before their marriage. He
would not expose her to the slightest shame.
Her virtue was too precious. Her name was
too sacred.

When he took Mary to be his wife, Joseph
was young and strong. He had a young body
and a loving heart. From his loving heart
came his purity. The vigor of youth did not
impede the perfect chastity with which he
guarded Mary's perpetual virginity. It rather gave it strength and joy.

In the Old Testament, the patriarch
Joseph protected the family of Jacob. From
Jacob and his twelves sons came Israel, the
Chosen People. Thus, he protected all of
Israel in its beginnings. Joseph in the New
Testament guarded and protected the fam-
ily of Nazareth which was the Church at
its beginnings. For the Church is the mys-
tical Body of Christ. It is all those joined in
faith and in the Holy Spirit to Christ. It is

the family of all those who believe in Him. Protecting Jesus, the head of the Church, and Mary, the first of all believers, Joseph protected the Church at its conception.

The Joseph of the Old Testament has the great dignity of saving the people of Egypt from starving from a severe famine. In the seven years of plenty, he had safely stored the grain. When the years of scarcity oppressed the people, Pharaoh told them, "Go to Joseph" (Gen 41:55). "But the second Joseph has a more excellent dignity than the first, seeing that the first gave to the Egyptians bread only for the body, but the second was, on behalf of all the elect, the watchful guardian of that Living Bread which came down from Heaven, of which whosoever eats will never die" (St. Bernardine of Siena, Sermon on St. Joseph).

Just as Joseph of Egypt was entrusted with the whole of Pharaoh's kingdom, so Joseph of Nazareth is now entrusted with the whole of God's kingdom. He is the Patron of Families and the Universal Church. To those whose souls are empty, to those whose hearts are burdened, to those with an uncertain future, to spouses and to children, to families broken and torn, the

Church repeats the words of Scripture: "Go to Joseph." "After the Mother of God, St. Joseph is, of all the saints, the one dearest to God. He has, therefore, great power with him..." (St. Alphonse Liguori).

> *Joseph was the guardian, the administrator and the legitimate and natural defender of the divine household of which he was the head... It is, then, natural and worthy that as the Blessed Joseph ministered to all the needs of the family at Nazareth and girt it about with his protection, he should now cover with the cloak of his heavenly patronage and defend the Church of Jesus Christ.*
>
> Pope Leo XIII, *Quamquam Pluries, 3*

CLOSING PRAYERS

To thee, O blessed Joseph, we have recourse in our affliction, and having implored the help of thy holy Spouse, we now, with hearts filled with confidence, earnestly beg thee also to take us under thy protection. By that charity where thou were united to the Immaculate Virgin Mother of God, and by that fatherly love with which thou did cherish the Child Jesus, we beseech thee and we humbly pray that thou will look down with gracious eyes upon that inheritance which Jesus Christ purchased by His blood, and will succor us in our need by thy power and strength.

Defend, O most watchful guardian of the Holy Family, the chosen offspring of Jesus Christ. Keep from us, O most loving Father, all blight of error and corruption. Aid us from on high, most valiant defender, in this conflict with the powers of darkness. And even as of old thou did rescue the Child Jesus from the peril of His life, so now defend God's Holy Church from the snares of the enemy and from all adversity. Shield us ever under thy patronage, that, following thy example and strengthened by thy help, we may live a holy life, die a happy death, and attain to everlasting bliss in Heaven. Amen.

Pope Leo XIII

Prayer for a Special Intention

O Blessed St. Joseph, tenderhearted Father, faithful guardian of Jesus, chaste spouse of the Mother of God,
I pray and beseech thee to offer to God the Father,

His Divine Son, bathed in Blood on the
    Cross for sinners,
and through the Holy Name of Jesus,
obtain for us from the Eternal Father, the
    favor I implore . . . Amen.

Memorare to St. Joseph

Remember, O most chaste spouse of the
Virgin Mary, that never was it known that
anyone who implored your help and sought
your intercession was left unassisted. Full
of confidence in your power I fly unto
you and beg your protection. Despise not
O Guardian of the Redeemer my humble
supplication, but in your bounty, hear and
answer me. Amen.

Our Father, Hail Mary, Glory be.

For additional prayers to St. Joseph see p. 87

Additional Prayers to St. Joseph

Litany of St. Joseph

Lord, have mercy on us
Christ, have mercy on us.
Lord, have mercy on us.
Christ, hear us,
Christ, graciously hear us.
God the Father of heaven,
have mercy on us.
God the Son, Redeemer of the World, have mercy on us.
God the Holy Spirit, have mercy on us.
Holy Trinity, one God, have mercy on us.
Holy Mary, pray for us.
St. Joseph, pray for us.
Renowned offspring of David, pray for us.
Light of Patriarchs, pray for us.
Spouse of the Mother of God, pray for us.
Chaste guardian of the Virgin, pray for us.
Foster father of the Son of God, pray for us.
Diligent protector of Christ, pray for us.
Head of the Holy Family, pray for us.
Joseph most just, pray for us.
Joseph most chaste, pray for us.
Joseph most prudent, pray for us.
Joseph most strong, pray for us.

Joseph most obedient, pray for us.
Joseph most faithful, pray for us.
Mirror of patience, pray for us.
Lover of poverty, pray for us.
Model of workers, pray for us.
Glory of home life, pray for us.
Guardian of virgins, pray for us.
Pillar of families, pray for us.
Solace of the afflicted, pray for us.
Hope of the sick, pray for us.
Patron of the dying, pray for us.
Terror of demons, pray for us.
Protector of Holy Church, pray for us.
Lamb of God, who take away the sins of the
    world, *spare us, O Lord.*
Lamb of God, who take away the sins of the
    world, *graciously hear us, O Lord.*
Lamb of God, who take away the sins of the
    world, *have mercy on us, O Lord.*

℣. He made him master of his house.
℟. *And lord over all his possessions.*

Let us pray

O God, in your ineffable providence you
were pleased to choose Blessed Joseph to be
the spouse of your most holy Mother; grant,
we beg you, that we may be worthy to have
him for our intercessor in heaven whom on

earth we venerate as our Protector: You who live and reign forever and ever.

Act of Consecration to St. Joseph

O dearest St. Joseph, I consecrate myself to your honor and give myself to you, that you may always be my father, my protector and my guide in the way of salvation.

Obtain for me a greater purity of heart and fervent love of the interior life.

After your example may I do all my actions for the greater glory of God, in union with the Divine Heart of Jesus and the Immaculate Heart of Mary.

O Blessed St. Joseph, pray for me, that I may share in the peace and joy of your holy death. Amen.

Traditional Prayer to St. Joseph

Oh St. Joseph whose protection is so great, so strong, so prompt before the throne of God, I place in you all my interests and desires. Oh St. Joseph do assist me by your powerful intercession and obtain for me from your divine son all spiritual blessings through Jesus Christ, our Lord; so that having engaged here below your heavenly power I may offer my thanksgiving and homage to the most loving of fathers. Oh St. Joseph, I never weary contemplating you and Jesus asleep in your arms. I dare not approach while he reposes near your heart. Press him in my name and kiss his fine head for me, and ask him to return the kiss when I draw my dying breath. St. Joseph, patron of departing souls, pray for us. Amen.

Prayer to Saint Joseph
for a Happy Death

O BLESSED Joseph, you gave forth your last breath in the loving embrace of Jesus and Mary. When the seal of death shall end my life, come with Jesus and Mary to aid me. Obtain for me this solace for that hour— to die with their holy arms around me.

Jesus, Mary, and Joseph, I commend my soul, living and dying, into your sacred arms.

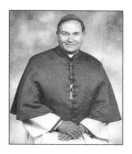

Bishop Emeritus Arthur J. Serratelli was the seventh bishop of the Diocese of Paterson, N.J. He is present chairman for the Vatican's Dialogue between the Catholic Church and the World Alliance of Baptists. He has served as chairman of the International Commission on English in the Liturgy; member of the Vatican's Congregation of Divine Worship and the Discipline of the Sacraments; and member of Vox Clara. He has served a three-year term as chairman of the Committee for the Translation of Sacred Scripture of the United States Conference of Catholic Bishops; twice chairman of the Committee on Divine Worship of the United States Conference of Catholic Bishops; chairman of the Committee on Doctrine; and member of the Subcommittee for the Review of Catechetical Texts. As a Professor of Sacred Scripture and Systematics, he has taught in three major seminaries. He continues to give retreats, lectures, and courses in Sacred Scripture as well as doing pastoral work in a parish.

This is the Bishop's fifth book. His previous books are: *From the Cross to the Empty Tomb, The Seven Gifts of the Holy Spirit, Jesus' Last Days,* and *The Parables of Jesus.*

JESUS' LAST DAYS

Most Rev. Arthur J. Serratelli, S.T.D., S.S.L., D.D.

The Cross was part of God's plan to bring Jesus to glory; and, it remains the instrument of our salvation. The Cross still speaks to the believer. For this reason, I offer the following biblical meditations on specific moments of the Passion narrative. In our own life, we  **are called to walk with Jesus in joy and in suffering. His Cross continues to enable us in every event of our life to discover God.**

A deeper understanding of the events of Jesus' last days as recorded in Scripture can help us to see more clearly our own call to discipleship today.

—From the Author's Introduction

Through Bishop Serratelli's reflections on the similar accounts of the four evangelists, we relive Jesus' Passion bathed in the light of Easter glory. We will appreciate how the Cross remains the instrument of our salvation and see more clearly our own call to discipleship. 128 pages. Size 5 x 7.

No. 932/04—Flexible cover... **6.95**
ISBN 978-1-9-47070-35-6

THE SEVEN GIFTS
OF THE HOLY SPIRIT

Most Rev. Arthur J. Serratelli, S.T.D., S.S.L., D.D.

Jesus alone possessed the seven gifts of the Holy Spirit in their fullness. But, the Holy Spirit graciously gives those same gifts to all who follow Jesus.

The seven gifts are our inheritance as baptized and confirmed Christians. We do not earn them. We do not merit them. They are given to us gratuitously. They make us open to the promptings of the Holy Spirit in our lives. They help us grow in holiness, making us fit for heaven. These seven gifts of the Holy Spirit help us live a truly authentic Christian way of life.

—*From the Author's Introduction*

Through history, art, Scripture, and Catholic documents, you will appreciate and grasp more fully how the seven gifts of the Holy Spirit can help you to live a truly authentic Christian life filled with peace and joy. 96 pages. Size 4 3/8 x 6 3/4.

No. 930/04—Flexible cover.............................. **5.95**
ISBN 978-1-947070-23-3

FROM THE CROSS TO THE EMPTY TOMB

Most Rev. Arthur J. Serratelli, S.T.D., S.S.L., D.D.

As Christians, we make our life-journey in union with Christ Crucified. The *Via Crucis* is the school of Christian life. As Peter once asked Jesus, the world questions each of us today, *"Quo Vadis?"* "Where are you going?" It will help each of us respond to this question by accompanying Jesus on the Way to the Cross. I offer the following brief meditations on individuals who were with Jesus in the last hours of His own life on earth.

—From the Author's Introduction

The author invites you to journey with those who were with Jesus in His last hours. You may be like Peter one day, and like Judas, Simon, Mary Magdalene, or Our Lady on another. This Lenten book provides a deeper appreciation for God's eternal saving love. 96 pages. Size 4 3/8 x 6 3/4.

No. 928/04—Flexible cover.. **6.95**
ISBN 978-1-947070-13-4

catholicbookpublishing.com

THE PARABLES OF JESUS

Most Rev. Arthur J. Serratelli, S.T.D., S.S.L., D.D.

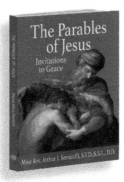

"Through the appeal of His parables and the grace they offer, Jesus is building up the kingdom of God. Those who do not believe in God are attempting to build a lasting city that will crumble and fall. But those who build upon the rock foundation of Jesus, the Eternal Word, can face the raging storms and winds of this world and remain secure unto eternity."

—*From the Conclusion*

Follow Jesus through His interaction with farmers, shepherds, aristocrats, religious and political leaders, and laborers in 13 parables filled with contrast, exaggeration, humor, and surprise that represent more than one third of His teachings. Both the scholar and student, the expert and the layperson can draw inspiration from the greatest storyteller the world has ever known. Even lifetime Catholics who think they know the parables will be rewarded with the wisdom and history that the author shares on these beloved, grace-filled stories. 176 pages. Size 5 1/4 x 7 3/4.

No. 934/04—Flexible cover.. **7.95**
ISBN 978-1-953152-08-4

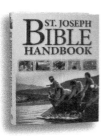

St. Joseph BIBLE HANDBOOK — In addition to a general introduction to each book of the Bible, the main headings found in every book—the *Outline, Frequently Asked Questions, Study Questions,* and *Look out for...*— succinctly point to the valuable information contained in the pages of the Bible. 256 pages. Size 6¾ x 9½.

No. 649/04—Durable cover **19.95**
ISBN 978-1-941243-98-5

St. Joseph NEW CATHOLIC BIBLE NEW TESTAMENT — This readable study edition has a large, easy-to-read typeface, complete notes and references, self-explaining maps, a handy Study Guide, a Bible Dictionary, the words of Christ in red, photographs, and many other features. Ideal for schools and Bible study. 528 pages. Size 6½ x 9¼.

No. 311/19—Burgundy Dura-Lux cover.......**17.95**
ISBN: 978-1-947070-66-0

DAY BY DAY WITH St. Joseph — By Msgr. Joseph Champlin and Msgr. Ken Lasch. Pray with St. Joseph every day of the year with a Scripture verse, short reflection, and prayer focusing on his deep faith, trust, and love for God, his family, and the Church. 192 pages. Size 4 x 6¼.

No. 162/19—Dura-Lux cover **9.95**
ISBN 978-1-937913-08-3

St. Joseph: MAN OF FAITH — By Jacques Gauthier. This book focuses on the excerpts of the New Testament in which St. Joseph appears, speaks of his veneration, and concludes with some prayers that will awaken our contemplative glance on this Patron of the Church and of workers. Illustrated. 96 pages. Size 4¼ x 6¾.

No. 72/04—Flexible cover **4.95**
ISBN 978-1-937913-94-6